A Parent's Guide

to the

Interscholastic Equestrian

Association

A Parent's Guide
to the
Interscholastic Equestrian
Association

By: Amanda Garner

Photographs by Kensie Arnold

ISBN: 978-0-9960736-2-2

Printed in the United States of America

Photographs by Kensie Arnold

∞This paper meets the requirements of ANSI/NISO Z39.48-1992 (Permanence of Paper)

For my parents

CONTENTS

PROLOGUE

Annie feels the butterflies flutter in her stomach as she waits at the in-gate with Coach Kelly by her side. Coach gives her an encouraging smile as she wipes her boots and checks her stirrup length one last time. The stocky chestnut quarter horse the high school freshman is about to ride for the very first time exhales gently under her as if to say, "just another day at the office."

"My two practice jumps went well," Annie thinks to herself, "I can handle this."

"Can you tell me your course one more time?" Coach Kelly asks.

"Outside line, single blue, inside line, roll back to red, to single yellow," she mouths quietly as she draws her course in the air with her crop.

"Good," her coach replies. "You can do this. Just relax and have fun," she says with a grin.

"Next in: Rider One-Thirty-Four. One-Three-Four," the announcer's voice crackles over the loud speaker.

Annie sees the in-gate person motioning to her. "You're next!" the gatekeeper beckons.

Annie takes a deep breath and guides her horse forward into the ring…

Congratulations! Your child has decided to join an Interscholastic Equestrian Association (IEA) equestrian team. Just like Annie, one day soon your young equestrian will find herself waiting at the in-gate for a turn in the ring.

But Annie's journey didn't start at the in-gate. It started months earlier when she first decided to join an IEA team…

FOREWORD

As an Interscholastic Equestrian Association (IEA) steward, I interact directly with coaches, show managers, administrative staff, riders, and parents and over the years I've fielded many questions from IEA riders and their parents. I decided to write this book to explain how the IEA works in a clear/concise manner in order to help parents and riders get the most from their IEA experience.

A few notes before we begin: I have chosen to refer to all riders with the feminine pronoun (she/her) simply for ease of writing. No disrespect is meant to our young gentlemen riders, and there are many in the IEA. Also, I have made every attempt to provide equal exposure to both the hunt seat and western disciplines. Any perceived bias toward either riding style is unintended. And I'd also like my readers to note that the information and content expressed in this book is solely that of the author, not the IEA. For official IEA rules and regulations, please consult the IEA rules and regulations located at www.rideiea.org.

It is my sincere hope that-at the conclusion of this book-you will feel you have gained a better understanding and appreciation of the IEA as an outstanding organization for young equestrians. I also welcome your comments. You will find my contact information in the *About the Author* section.

Amanda Garner

March, 2014

CHAPTER ONE

A BRIEF OVERVIEW

"Is this the Equestrian Team meeting?" Annie asks excitedly as she stands in the doorway of Ms. Taylor's English classroom. Its 3:15pm and school just got out. Annie heard there was an Equestrian Team meeting after school and decided to see what it was all about.

"Yes, you found us," replies Ms. Taylor. "Come in and take a seat, we're about to get started."

"Welcome to our first Equestrian Team meeting of the school year," begins Ms. Taylor. "I'm the faculty sponsor and standing at the back is Kelly Barker, our team coach."

Annie turns in her seat to see a woman in blue jeans and a polo shirt with a Lincoln High School Equestrian Team logo.

"Those of you returning from last year already know Coach Kelly, the owner of Autumn Gate Farm. She coaches our hunt seat and western teams at her farm."

"Excuse me, Ms. Taylor," Annie says as she raises her hand tentatively. *"I don't have a horse. Can I still be on the team?"*

"Of course," Coach Kelly responds enthusiastically. *"We're part of the IEA. All of the horses and tack are provided. No previous showing experience is required either. Students at all skill levels are welcome on our IEA Equestrian Team. Coach Kelly is going to come forward now and tell you all about it..."*

This chapter provides a brief overview of the structure of the IEA and how it all works. For those of you with no prior experience with the IEA, this chapter will give you the information you need to get started.

The Interscholastic Equestrian Association in a Nutshell

Membership in the IEA is open to all middle and high school students (Grades 6-12). All horses and tack are provided.

At the horse shows, the riders draw at random the horse they will ride in the show. It will more than likely be a horse they've never ridden before.

The horse shows offer different levels of competition separated by rider skill level, so each rider competes against other riders of similar experience and ability.

Riders take lessons with their team coach on lesson horses in order to prepare them for the experience of riding an unfamiliar horse in competition.

Riders and teams accumulate points during the regular season with the goal of qualifying for the regional, zone, and national finals at the end of the competition year.

Organizational Structure

The IEA is a national organization split into ten zones by geographical location. Some zones are further divided into regions, depending on the number of teams within the zone.

Many IEA teams are affiliated with a middle school or high school, though the IEA also permits farm teams made of up students who ride at the same barn, but don't attend the same school.

Each team has a designated team coach. Some teams that are associated with a school also have a designated faculty sponsor.

Team Coach

The team coach most often is not employed by the school. Instead, the coach operates as an independent contractor. Students pay the coach for his/her services (teaching the lessons; providing the riding facility, horses, and tack; trailering horses to the shows; coaching at shows). The amount paid to the coach for lessons, coaching at horseshows, and use of the horses is determined by the coach, and varies among teams.

Faculty Sponsor

The faculty sponsor is employed by the school and acts as a liaison among the riders, coach, school, and IEA. The faculty sponsor is often responsible for the administrative tasks associated with running the team including collecting money; submitting entries; tracking team points; and interacting with the show managers, zone chair, and IEA national leadership. Sometimes the faculty sponsor is compensated through the school, though in a limited number of cases the team provides the faculty sponsor with a small stipend. Some faculty sponsors operate on a purely volunteer basis. In the case of farm teams, the faculty sponsor role is usually filled either by the team coach or a parent.

Most teams also have some sort of booster club run by the parents that assists the coach and faculty sponsor with organizing the team, handling the money, and planning the horse shows.

Riding Disciplines

The IEA offers competition in two disciplines: hunt seat and western. The hunt seat discipline consists of two classes: Equitation over Fences and Equitation on the Flat. The western division also has two classes: Western Horsemanship and Western Reining. Teams may be hunt seat only, western only, or both hunt seat and western. A description of the classes offered in IEA competition and the required skill level for each can be found in Chapter 5: Class Placement.

Lessons

IEA riders take a set number of lessons with their team coach (one lesson per week is pretty standard for most teams). Students who have an outside trainer can continue to ride with him/her in addition to taking lessons with their IEA coach. Some coaches allow riders to take fewer team lessons if they are actively riding with an outside trainer.

The lessons are most often offered in a group format with three or four students riding at the same time and most lessons last about an hour. The riders are grouped according to skill level and riding discipline and the lessons are conducted using the team lesson horses and lesson tack. More information on lessons can be found in Chapter 4: Lessons.

Team Meetings

In addition to lessons, teams often hold meetings to discuss team business. These meetings may take place at the school or at the barn. Team

Booster Clubs also hold meetings periodically to discuss team business among the parents and other adult supporters.

Horse Shows

For someone unfamiliar with horse shows, the IEA competitions are structured similarly to a track or swim meet, with many events (called classes) taking place throughout the day and several teams competing against each other to win points based on their placings in each class. Each rider accumulates individual points and each team accumulates team points based on the placings in each class. At the end of the day the High Point and Reserve High Point Teams are determined based on the number of points won. An explanation of the point system is located in Chapter 7: Points and the Post Season.

The competitors ride horses supplied by the host team or brought by one of the visiting teams. The horses are drawn at random before the show begins. The draw is introduced in Chapter 6: Elements of an IEA Horse Show and explained in detail in Chapter 8: A Closer Look at the Draw.

Finding a Team

To find a team, prospective riders who attend a school with an existing equestrian team just need to contact either the faculty sponsor or team coach. Riders who would like to join a barn team should visit the official IEA website: www.rideiea.org for a list of stables offering barn teams not affiliated with a particular school.

If a prospective rider's school doesn't currently have a team, starting a new school team isn't as daunting as it sounds. The official IEA website has easy to follow instructions for forming a new team and the IEA administrative officials (Membership Marketing Coordinator and others on the national staff, zone chairs, region chairs, etc.) are more than happy to assist.

Registration

After finding an IEA team, the first step for new riders is to register as a member of the IEA for the competition year and pay the membership dues. A detailed explanation of the registration process for teams, coaches, riders, and contributing members can be found in Chapter 2: Registration.

CHAPTER TWO

REGISTRATION

"Wow, this is so confusing. What's the difference between an individual membership and a contributing membership?" Annie's mom mutters as she scrolls through the IEA website.

"Don't worry about it mom. Ms. Taylor will let you know what we need to do and what the costs are. She's the faculty sponsor. That's what she's there for." Annie replies. "It's no big deal. She does this every year and she's got it down pat."

IEA teams, coaches, and individual riders must register with the IEA each year and submit the required paperwork. This chapter provides a description of the required documents and fees and registration deadlines; however, a child's registration should be done in coordination with your team coach and/or faculty sponsor to ensure everything is done completely and correctly.

Please note that the fees and registration deadlines referenced in this chapter are for the 2013-2014 competition year. Copies of all the documents listed below as well as the current fees and deadlines can be found on the official IEA website www.rideiea.org.

There are four types of teams:

- Upper School Hunt Seat

- Upper School Western

- Middle School Hunt Seat

- Middle School Western

Each team must have a minimum of one coach and three riders in one of the four team types listed above.

For a team to be eligible to compete, the following documentation and fees must be submitted to the IEA National Membership office by November 15 of the competition year or two weeks prior to the team's first competition, whichever comes first. A team is considered complete and eligible for competition only when all necessary documentation has been submitted, accepted, and processed.

- Team Application Form

- Team Membership Dues

- At least three Rider Applications for each type of team joining

- Completed Rider Application/Waiver of Liability Forms containing all necessary signatures.

- Riders' Dues of $45 per rider per discipline per year

- Completed Coach Application/Waiver of Liability Form, Coach Dues of $50 total per year, regardless of whether the coach has teams competing in one discipline or both disciplines, and Proof of insurance (certificate stating named coach and appropriate equestrian instruction language) or Equisure Application and Payment (checks made payable to "IEA")

- Contributing membership dues (if applicable) of $45 per contributing member per year. Contributing Members are adult members of the IEA who are authorized to handle team communications and assist with paperwork with the coach's permission.

- Show hosting application

IEA coaches must be at least 21 years old and covered by a liability policy carrying a minimum coverage of $500,000 per occurrence. The IEA offers coverage through Equisure that can be purchased through the Membership Office. ($150/year covers participation in IEA events and practices)

IEA horse shows are hosted by IEA teams. In the first year or part year of competition, a team is not obligated to host/co-host an IEA competition. In the second year of competition, a team must co-host a minimum of one IEA competition. In the third year of competition and each year thereafter, a team must co-host two or host one IEA regular season point show as the Event Host Coordinator (EHC).

If two or more IEA members and/or coach from the previous year form a team they are considered a returning team and must fulfill all hosting obligations.

In addition to the required documentation and fees listed above all, coaches and contributing member team organizers must have read and be familiar with the current IEA Rulebook

Once your team's membership packet has been submitted and accepted by the IEA membership office, you're officially registered as a team and eligible to compete.

CHAPTER THREE

WHAT TO WEAR

"$300.00 for a show helmet?!?" Annie's mom exclaims as they examine the wide variety of helmets at the local tack store. "Is this really necessary? Can't you just wear your schooling helmet with a velvet cover?"

"Hey mom, that's a bargain," Annie replies, "Rachel said her mom paid almost $500.00 for her western show slinky since it was custom made. But I also heard that Kristie's mom found some great deals on breeches and show jackets online, so we can look there too for the other things I need."

In the IEA, the horses and tack are provided, but the students must furnish their own lesson and show attire.

Lesson Attire

Every coach has their own requirements for lesson attire. Some coaches are very formal, expecting their students to wear breeches and tall boots to their lessons, while others are more laid back, allowing paddock boots and half-chaps. On the western side, most coaches prefer blue jeans and boots with a heel.

Either way, your child's lesson clothing should be clean and well-fitted and her shirt should be tucked in. It is difficult for a trainer to evaluate a rider's position if she is wearing an oversized baggy shirt.

Regarding helmets, riders have the option of wearing their show helmet or a schooling helmet for lessons. A schooling helmet is appropriate as long as it is ASTM/SEI approved. Please note, helmets protect the rider's head in a fall by breaking to absorb the impact, so helmets should be thoroughly inspected and possibly replaced after any fall in which the rider's head hits the ground.

Below is a list of recommended attire for hunt seat and western lessons.

Lesson Attire—Hunt Seat

- Paddock boots and half-chaps or tall boots
- Riding breeches or blue jeans
- Well-fitted tucked in shirt
- Gloves
- Belt
- Hairnet
- ASTM/SEI Approved Helmet

Lesson Attire—Western

- Boots with a heel

- Blue jeans or riding pants

- Well-fitted tucked in shirt

- ASTM/SEI Approved Helmet*

*Helmets are optional for western riding unless required by the coach or by state law. For example, New York state law requires all persons under the age of fourteen to wear an ASTM/SEI approved helmet when mounted.

Examples of hunt seat and western lesson attire

Horse Show Attire

Dressing for success is just as important in the show ring as it is in the business world. Judges will say they are evaluating the ride and not the outfit, but a hunt seat rider who walks in the ring wearing a top-of-the-line helmet looks like the winner while a rider wearing tall boots that are two inches too short doesn't. On the western side, a rider with a well-fitting and properly shaped western hat looks sharp while a rider with a misshapen hat that flies off her head at the lope looks sloppy.

Wearing the right clothing becomes more important the higher the division. For example, a beginner rider may be fine in a schooling helmet with a velvet cover, while a varsity open rider would not. A beginner western rider can get away with chaps that are a bit "frumpy" while a varsity open rider should wear chaps tailored to her shape.

First and foremost, no matter which level of competition, your child's show clothes should be clean and fit well. This includes making sure they are dry-cleaned regularly. Also, each type of competition has its own standards for show attire. From a hunt seat perspective, the IEA tends to follow the fashion trends found at United States Equestrian Federation (USEF) competitions. On the western side, riders tend to model their dress on what is seen in the American Quarter Horse Association (AQHA) and the National Reigning Horse Association (NRHA) show pens.

The IEA, as well as other western riding associations such as the AQHA and NRHA currently do not have a rule requiring helmets in western competition. Some coaches require helmets for western lessons, but allow riders to wear traditional western hats at shows; others require helmets at all times; and others don't require helmets at all. As noted, some state laws require riders under a certain age to wear helmets, at all times, when mounted.

At western horse shows, judges are not allowed to penalize a rider for choosing to wear an ASTM/SEI approved helmet and all riders are given the option to wear a helmet.

Below is a list of appropriate hunt seat and western show attire.

Hunt Seat Show Attire

- Dark hunt coat—navy or black
- Beige or tan hunt seat britches with knee patches
- White or light pastel show shirt with collar (female riders)
- White or conservatively colored button down dress shirt with neck tie (male riders)
- Tall boots
- Black gloves
- ASTM/SEI-approved helmet
- Hairnet (female riders)
- Belt

For proper fit, tall boots should come up to the back of the knee. They will drop when they're worn in, so you should buy them a little too tall.

The hunt coat should fit snugly in order to show the rider's position. If the coat is too big or baggy, it can make the rider look loose or unkempt.

Younger riders (generally 12 years and under) may wear jodhpurs with garter straps and paddock boots instead of breeches and tall boots. Riders in jodhpurs may also wear their hair braided with bows rather than contained in a helmet with a hair net.

Examples of appropriate hunt seat show attire

The following should not be worn in hunt seat shows:

Full-Seat breeches (dressage breeches)—While technically not prohibited, they look out of place in hunt seat competition.

Stock Pins—while considered appropriate for dressage competition and in hunt seat competition in some breed association shows, most judges consider stock pins unconventional in hunt seat equitation competition.

Half-Chaps—again, this is a case where a lower level rider (beginner) may be able to get away with it, whereas an upper level rider would not.

Show Bows—as stated above regarding stock pins, show bows may be standard for dressage and breed show competition, but they are considered unconventional in hunt seat equitation competition. Hunter hair neatly contained in a hair net is more appropriate.

Western Show Attire

- Western show top or vest (female riders)

- Button down shirt with neck scarf (male riders)

- Show pants or jeans

- Chaps

- Boots

- Western hat or helmet

- Spurs (except beginners)

- Hair in bun with hairnet (horsemanship classes)

- Hair in a neat pony tail (optional for reining classes)

Western horsemanship attire
with slinky show top and hair in bun with hairnet

Reining attire with button down shirt and hair in pony tail

Novice, Intermediate, and Open western horsemanship riders should purchase their own pair of ball spurs. This is because the spur must fit the rider's boot correctly in order to stay in place during the ride. Beginner riders are not allowed to wear spurs.

In some cases, reining riders are allowed to wear a rowelled spur. If so, the rowelled spur will be supplied by the horse provider, thus riders do not need to invest in their own pair of rowelled spurs.

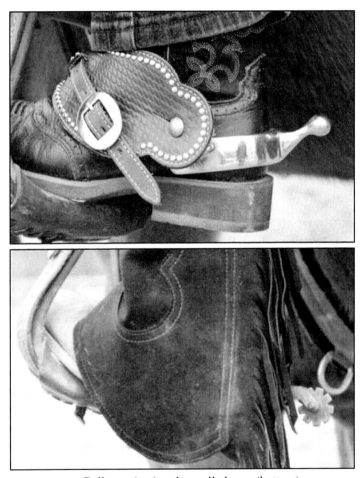

Ball spur (top) and rowelled spur (bottom)

CHAPTER FOUR

LESSONS

Annie inhales the rich, familiar aroma of horses and hay as she walks though the big barn doors. She's a little early for her first lesson and stands nervously in the barn aisle clutching her helmet while looking around for a friendly face.

"Hi there, you must be Annie."

Annie turns quickly towards the welcoming voice.

"I'm Stacy, one of Coach Kelly's working students. I'll help you get ready for your lesson."

"Thanks!" Annie replies with relief, "this is my first day here and I don't really know what I'm supposed to do."

"No problem," the older girl answers. "Let's check the white board to see who you're riding and then I'll show you where we keep the tack and grooming supplies."

As noted previously, IEA riders take a set number of lessons with their team coach (one lesson per week is pretty standard for most teams). Students who have an outside trainer can continue to ride with him/her in addition to the required lessons with their IEA coach. Some coaches allow riders to take fewer team lessons if they are actively riding with an outside trainer.

The lessons are most often offered in a group format with three or four students riding at the same time and most lessons last about an hour. The riders are grouped according to skill level and riding discipline and the lessons are conducted using the team lesson horses and lesson tack.

Get There Early

The assigned lesson time is the time when your child should be tacked up and in the ring, not just arriving at the barn. It's a good idea to get to the barn about a half-hour before the scheduled lesson time. Once your child gets to know the horses and the barn routine you can adjust your

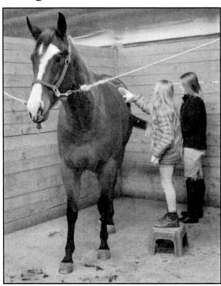

arrival time accordingly. If she is new to riding or inexperienced in tacking up, the coach will designate someone to help her get the horse groomed and ready for the lesson.

Some coaches write the riders' names next to the horse they are assigned to ride on a white board hanging in the barn aisle. Others are more informal, just telling the riders when they arrive which horse they will be riding.

Two students preparing for their lesson

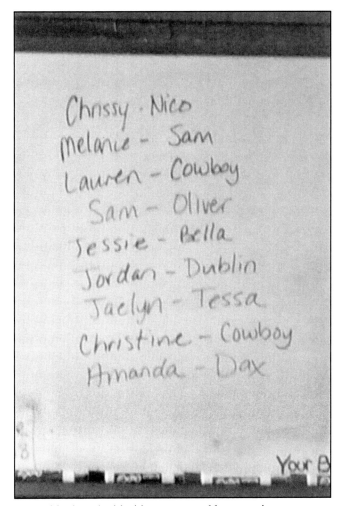

White board with rider names and horse assignments

Ride a Variety of Different Horses

In IEA horse shows, competitors are required to ride horses they've probably never ridden before in unfamiliar tack with little or no warm-up. To prepare for this the coaches have their students ride a variety of horses in their lessons, from the 14.1 hand pony to the 17 hand draft horse, and from the twenty year old quarter horse to the six year old off the track thoroughbred. Horses come in all shapes and sizes (and temperaments!) and IEA riders must be proficient in riding all of them.

Most IEA lessons, hunt seat and western, are held in groups

Ride in a Variety of Tack

In addition to riding an unfamiliar horse, in IEA horse shows the competitors must ride in the tack provided with the horse. To prepare for this, the coaches have their students ride in a variety of tack. Most equestrians would agree that it is more difficult to ride a familiar horse in an unfamiliar saddle than an unfamiliar horse in familiar tack.

Hunt Seat Tack

In the hunt seat discipline, most of the saddles will be close contact hunt seat saddles, but they will differ on knee rolls, knee and thigh blocks, leather quality, and seat size and depth. Students should be comfortable riding in padded saddles with knee rolls as well as flat as a pancake saddles with no knee rolls or blocks.

Various hunt seat saddles

Also, there are many different styles of stirrup irons including standard fillis stirrups, peacock safety stirrups, and flex stirrups. It is important for students to spend time riding in each of these because stirrup type can affect leg position and base of support.

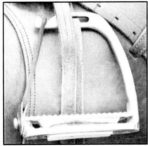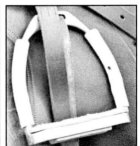

Various stirrup types: Fillis (left), peacock (middle), and flex (right)

Coaches also have their riders practice riding with double reins because some horses at the shows are ridden in a pelham.

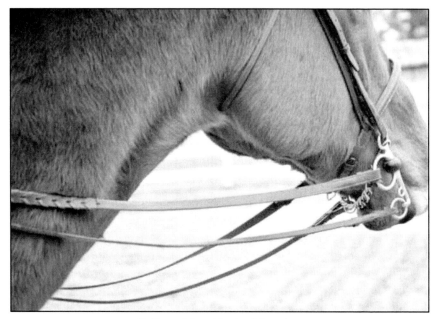

Pelham bit with double reins

Western Tack

Western saddles also come in a variety of styles and sizes. Unlike hunt seat saddles, the stirrups on western saddles cannot be rolled to make them shorter. At the horse shows, if the stirrups won't shorten enough for a rider, the coach can request a tack change from the steward. Many coaches bring smaller saddles with them to the horse shows to be prepared in case this happens.

Various western saddles

With regards to bridles and bits, western horses can be ridden one-handed or two-handed, as designated by the horse provider on the horse description sheet. Ideally, horses wearing a snaffle bit should be ridden two-handed and those wearing a shank bit should be ridden one-handed. Coaches have their riders practice riding both ways in their lessons to prepare for both scenarios.

Two handed with snaffle bit (above) and one handed with shank bit (below)

Lesson Format

The lessons are tailored to each rider's competition level. Riders who compete only in hunt seat flat will spend most of their lesson time working on flat work while riders who compete over fences will spend time working over fences in addition to flat work. On the western side, riders who compete only in horsemanship classes will spend their lesson time focusing on rail work while reining riders will devote a number of lessons to practicing the intricate components of the reining pattern.

Requirements for Showing

IEA rules require all students to have a minimum of one year of continuous professional instruction before competing in their first IEA show.

CHAPTER FIVE

CLASS PLACEMENT

"Can you tell me a little bit about your riding experience, Annie?"
Coach Kelly asks. I need to place you in your showing division and I
want to make sure we place you fairly.

"Well, I've been taking lessons at a small barn for a couple of years.
Most of the time I jump about 2'3" to 2'6" on my favorite lesson horse,
Buster. We've done a few shows together. Nothing too high, just long
stirrup at the local saddle club shows." Annie replies.

"That's great Annie!" Coach Kelly replies. "Since you've had more
than one year of instruction over fences and you're comfortable jumping
2'3"to 2'6" on a familiar horse, I'm going to place you into Junior
Varsity Novice Equitation on the Flat and Over Fences Crossrails."

The team coach places the riders in their appropriate divisions
based on their previous riding and showing experience. Below is an
excerpt from the 2013-2014 IEA rulebook listing the different

divisions and the recommended rider skill level for each. The hunt seat and western rider tests referenced in the class descriptions are listed following the class descriptions.

In the hunt seat discipline, riders are placed into two classes; a fence class and a flat class, unless they are at the beginner level, in which case they are placed only in the beginner flat class. In the western discipline, intermediate and open riders are placed into two classes; a horsemanship class and a reining class, while novice and beginner riders are placed only in a horsemanship class.

As you read through the divisions, please note that riders should be placed in divisions (particularly fence heights) that are lower than the level at which the rider is capable of competing on their own horse (or a horse they ride regularly). This is because, as noted in a previous chapter, in IEA competition the riders are asked to compete on an unfamiliar horse with little or no warm-up.

Hunt Seat Equitation over Fences Classes

Class 1: Varsity Open Equitation o/f 2'6"—Riders should be capable of jumping 3'-3'6" on their usual mounts at home. Riders may have shown in any horse show, recognized or unrecognized, at 3'3" or above. Coaches should be confident these riders could safely perform over a 2'6" Hunter or equitation course on an unfamiliar horse. Riders participating in Varsity Open over Fences are expected to compete throughout the season in Varsity Open Flat. To be eligible for post season competitions (individual or team) riders must have accumulated the required points and participated in a minimum of two (2) Varsity Open Flat classes during the regular season.

Class 2: Varsity Intermediate Equitation o/f 2' – Riders should be capable of jumping 2'6"-3' on their usual mounts at home. Intermediate Riders may have shown in any horse show, recognized or unrecognized, at 3' or below. Riders who have won 10 or more blue ribbons at 3' must be placed in Varsity Open O/F. Coaches should be confident these riders would be able to safely perform over 2' Hunter or equitation course on an unfamiliar horse. Riders participating in Varsity Intermediate over Fences are expected to compete throughout the season in Varsity Intermediate or Varsity Open Flat. To be eligible for post season competitions (individual or team), riders must have accumulated the required points and participated in a minimum of two (2) Varsity Intermediate or Varsity Open Flat classes during the regular season.

Class 3: Junior Varsity Novice Equitation o/f x-rails – Riders should be capable of jumping 2'-2'6" on their usual mounts at home. Junior Varsity Novice Riders may have shown in any horse show, recognized or unrecognized, at 2'6" or below. Riders who have won 10 or more blue ribbons at 2'6" must be placed in the next higher appropriate level. Riders should have a minimum of one year of professional instruction over fences. Coaches should be confident these riders would be able to safely perform over an x-rails Hunter or equitation course on an unfamiliar horse. Riders participating in Junior Varsity Novice over Fences are expected to compete throughout the season in Junior Varsity Novice or Varsity Intermediate Flat. To be eligible for post season competitions (individual or team), riders must have accumulated the required points and participated in a minimum of two (2) Junior Varsity Novice or Varsity Intermediate Flat classes during the regular season.

Class 4: Future Intermediate Equitation o/f 2' – Restricted to middle school riders who meet the criteria for Hunt Seat Class 2. Riders participating in Future Intermediate over Fences are expected to compete throughout the season in Future Intermediate Flat. To be eligible for post season competitions (individual or team), riders must have accumulated the required points and participated in a minimum of two (2) Future Intermediate Flat classes during the regular season.

Class 5: Future Novice o/f x-rails - Restricted to middle school riders who meet the criteria for Hunt Seat Class 3. Riders participating in Future Novice over Fences are expected to compete throughout the season in Future Novice or Future Intermediate Flat. To be eligible for post season competitions (individual or team), riders must have accumulated the required points and participated in a minimum of two (2) Future Novice or Future Intermediate Flat classes during the regular season.

Hunt Seat Equitation on the Flat Classes

Riders without jumping experience should be assessed according to their ability to perform flatwork tests, as listed in Rule 3305.

Class 6: Varsity Open Equitation on the flat – These riders should be capable of performing Hunt Seat Tests 1 through 13.

Class 7: Varsity Intermediate Equitation on the flat – These riders should be capable of performing Hunt Seat Tests 1 through 9.

Class 8: Junior Varsity Novice Equitation on the flat – These riders should be capable of performing Hunt Seat Tests 1 through 8.

Class 9: Junior Varsity Beginner Equitation on the flat Walk/ Trot/Canter – Open to riders who are not eligible for Novice level jumping classes, but should be experienced enough to canter an unfamiliar animal in a group. These riders should be capable of performing Hunt Seat Tests 1 through 7. A Beginner rider may not have shown over fences larger than 2' in any horse show. To be eligible for Class 9, a rider must have had at least one year continuous professional instruction, must demonstrate proficiency at the trot and canter, and be capable of competing on a variety of unfamiliar horses. A Walk/Trot class is an optional offering and is open only to those riders competing in the Walk/Trot/Canter class. Entry fees will be collected but no individual or team points will be awarded. The intent is not to accommodate lower level riders. Competitors in W/T must meet eligibility requirements of Hunt Seat Class 9 and must compete in the W/T/C class.

Class 9x: Walk/Trot – (optional offering and does not count for points) Open only to those riders who are riding in Class 9: Junior Varsity Beginner Equitation on the flat Walk/Trot/ Canter.

Class 10: Future Intermediate Equitation on the flat – Restricted to middle school riders who are capable of performing Hunt Seat Tests 1 through 9.

Class 11: Future Novice Equitation on the flat – Restricted to middle school riders who are capable of performing Hunt Seat Tests 1 through 8.

Class 12: Future Beginner Equitation on the flat Walk/Trot/ Canter – Restricted to middle school riders who meet the eligibility requirements of Class 9.

Class 12x: Walk/Trot—(optional offering and does not count for points) Open only to those riders who are riding in Class 12: Future Beginner Equitation on the Flat Walk/Trot/Canter.

Varsity Open Championship Class – The top Varsity Open riders as determined by points and places within the show are eligible for this class. The class requires a minimum of six (6) riders, and should be limited to the top ten (10). Riders must be eligible to complete in Varsity Open over Fences (2'6") to be eligible for this championship class. The class may be run using the same mount for both phases of the competition, or a separate draw may be done for each phase. The judge may choose to implement any additional testing after the completion of the two mandatory phases. Phase 1 – Riders will be judged over an advanced equitation course with jumps from 2'6" to 3'. Hunt Seat tests 1-13 may be asked. Phase 2 – Riders will also compete on the Flat and may be asked to perform any of tests 1-11.

Hunt Seat Rider Tests

A rider must be prepared to perform the test appropriate for the class in which the rider is participating. Riders may be requested to perform the following tests collectively or individually during a show or competition. No other tests may be used. The judge may choose only from the following list and instructions for performance of the test must be publicly announced:

1. Asked an appropriate horsemanship question that is tailored to the rider's ability level
2. Halt
3. Sitting trot
4. Two point position at the walk and/or trot
5. Figure eight at trot, demonstrating change of diagonals
6. Figure eight at canter on correct lead, demonstrating simple change of lead
7. Change Horses
8. Ride without stirrups
9. Change leads down center of ring demonstrating simple change of lead
10. Canter on the counter lead. No more than eight horses may counter canter at one time
11. Half-turn on forehand and/or half-turn on haunches
12. Jump a shortened course
13. Trot a jump not to exceed 2'6".

Western Horsemanship Classes

Class 1: Varsity Open Horsemanship—Riders who have competed at nationally qualifying competitions such as, but not limited to, youth team or world show qualifying competitions, also, riders who have won NRHA or AQHA world top 5 placing or any rider with a top 5 placing at the All American Quarter Horse Congress, Paint, Appaloosa, and other breed show equivalents. Showmanship, halter, hunt seat, and contest classes are excluded. Riders who have finished in the top ten in a nationally recognized breed or world show competition (QH Congress, AQHA, NRHA, APHA, ApHC, PtHA) in a western mounted class; and/or riders who finished in the top two year-end standings in a recognized state breed association or top ten national ranking for year end results. This excludes games, halter, showmanship, walk trot, and 10 & under. These riders should be capable of performing western horsemanship tests 1-10.

Class 2: Varsity Intermediate Horsemanship—These riders are those who have won 5 or more blue ribbons in Western horsemanship or reining in breed or National Reining Horse associations, for example: Quarter Horse, Paint, and Appaloosa and NRHA shows. Riders who have won five (5) or more blue ribbons in western mounted classes at nationally recognized breed association competitions, (i.e. AQHA, APHA, NRHA, ApHC, PtHA) OR have earned twenty-two (22) or more total points from a breed association in western classes (including novice divisions) excluding halter, showmanship, games, walk-trot, and 10 & under. These riders should be capable of performing Western Horsemanship tests 1-8.

Class 3: Junior Varsity Novice Horsemanship—These riders may have shown at open shows and non-breed specific shows, for example, 4H events and county fairs. Riders who have shown at more than eight (8) open shows or county fairs and have not won five (5) blue ribbons in a western mounted class at a nationally recognized breed association show. (i.e. AQHA, APHA, NRHA, ApHC, PtHA) These riders have earned less than twenty-two (22) total points in any breed association in western classes (including novice divisions). This excludes halter, showmanship, games, walk-trot, and 10 & under. These riders should be capable of performing Western Horsemanship tests 1-6.

Class 4: Junior Varsity Beginner Horsemanship—Open to riders who are not eligible for Novice level classes, but should be experienced enough to walk, jog and lope an unfamiliar animal in a group. These riders should be capable of performing Western tests 1-6 and may have participated in camp shows and in-house farm shows. Riders may not have shown at a lope in more than five (5) eight (8) open shows (i.e. 4H events and county fairs) and non-breed specific shows. IEA experience at the Beginner level in a different discipline does not count. To be eligible for class 4, riders must have at least one year continuous professional instruction, must demonstrate proficiency at a jog and lope, and must be capable of competing on a variety of unfamiliar horses. A Walk/Jog class is an optional offering and is open only to those riders competing in the Walk/Jog/Lope class. Entry fees will be collected but no individual or team points will be awarded. The intent is not to accommodate lower level riders. Competitors in Walk/Jog must meet eligibility requirements of Western Class 4 and must compete in the Walk/Jog/Lope class.

Class 4x: Walk/Jog—(optional offering and does not count for points) Open only to those riders who are riding in Class 4: Junior Varsity Beginner Horsemanship.

Class 5: Future Intermediate Horsemanship—Restricted to middle school riders who meet the criteria for Western Horsemanship Class 2 and/or are capable of performing Western Horsemanship tests 1-8.

Class 6: Future Novice Horsemanship—Restricted to middle school riders who meet the criteria for Western Horsemanship Class 3 and/or who are capable of performing Western Horsemanship tests 1-6.

Class 7: Future Beginner Horsemanship—Restricted to middle school riders who meet the criteria for Western Horsemanship Class 4. These riders should be capable of performing Western Horsemanship tests 1-6.

Class 7x: Walk/Jog—(optional offering and does not count for points) Open only to those riders who are riding in Class 7: Future Beginner Horsemanship.

Western Reining Classes

Class 8: Varsity Open Reining—Restricted to those riders competing in the Varsity Open Horsemanship. Riders participating in Varsity Open Reining are expected to compete throughout the season in Varsity Open Horsemanship. To be eligible for post season competitions (individual or team) riders must have accumulated the required points and participated in a minimum of two (2) Varsity Open Horsemanship classes during the regular season. Riders should have a minimum of one-year professional reining instruction.

Class 9: Varsity Intermediate Reining—Restricted to riders competing in Varsity Intermediate or Varsity Open Horsemanship. Riders participating in Varsity Intermediate Reining are expected to compete throughout the season in Varsity Intermediate or Varsity Open Horsemanship. To be eligible for post season competitions (individual or team) riders must have accumulated the required points and participated in a minimum of two (2) Varsity Intermediate or Varsity OpenHorsemanship classes during the regular season. Riders should have a minimum of one-year professional reining instruction.

Class 10: Future Intermediate Reining—Restricted to riders competing in the Future Intermediate Horsemanship Class. Riders participating in Future Intermediate Reining are expected to compete throughout the season in Future Intermediate Horsemanship. To be eligible for post season competitions (individual or team) riders must have accumulated the required points and participated in a minimum of two (2) Future Intermediate Horsemanship classes during the regular season. Riders should have a minimum of one-year professional reining instruction.

Championship Western Award—This is an award issued to the high point rider based on the total of the Varsity Open Horsemanship and Varsity Open Reining points. In case of a tie, the judge(s) may require a ride off, the type of which to be determined by each judge.

Western Horsemanship Tests

A Western judge may choose from the following horsemanship tests. Any one or combination of appropriate or equivalent tests may be used:

1. Ask an appropriate horsemanship question that is tailored to the rider's ability level

2. Individual performance on the rail

3. Halt and/or back

4. Figure eight at the jog

5. Change horses

6. Lope on specific lead and stop

7. 360 degree turn

8. Figure eight at the lope, demonstrating a change of lead (through the walk or jog)

9. Ride without stirrups

10. Simple change of leads in a straight line.

Pointing Up

Once a rider meets certain benchmarks, she will be required to advance to the next higher division. This is commonly referred to as "pointing up." The benchmarks for pointing up are described in the paragraphs below.

Riders may not compete in the same division for more than two show seasons. After two seasons, she is required to move up to the next higher division. However, if a coach feels that a rider should not advance to the next division after two show seasons, he/she may file a petition with IEA asking that the rider be evaluated by the show steward at that rider's first IEA show of the new season. The steward then makes a determination either to keep the rider at the higher level or allow the rider to drop back down to the previous lower level.

If a rider accumulates twenty-two points in a class in any single competition year, that rider must move up at least one division at the beginning of the next competition year.

If a rider earns twenty-two points in equitation on the flat or western horsemanship during the show season, but not in equitation over fences or reining, she is required to move up to the next higher division in flat or horsemanship, but may remain in her current fences or reining division. However, a rider who advances in equitation over fences or reining must also advance in equitation on the flat or western horsemanship. Thus, a rider is allowed to compete in a higher flat or horsemanship division than fence or reining division, but is not allowed to compete in a higher fence or reining division than flat or horsemanship division.

Rider points are not carried over from one year to the next.

Any rider who has qualified or shown as an individual rider in the previous season's national finals must advance to the next division the following season. However, riders selected to compete in team classes at the national finals who do not meet any of the other advancement criteria are not required to advance to the next division the following season.

All middle school riders graduating to upper school competition should be reevaluated as "initial placements" and assigned to the appropriate division.

CHAPTER SIX

MAJOR PLAYERS AND ELEMENTS OF AN IEA HORSE SHOW

"Hey Coach, do you have a minute?" Annie asks as she dismounts from her lesson horse and runs up her stirrups.

"Sure, Annie, what's on your mind?"

"I'm really nervous about my first IEA show next week. I know I've done lots of shows with my old barn, but that was on my favorite lesson horse that I rode every week. I've never been to a show where I have to ride a horse I've never ridden before."

"You've got nothing to worry about, Annie," Coach Kelly reassures her. "You'll get to watch the morning schooling and we'll read the horse description together to make sure we have a good idea of who you're

going to ride. And I'm willing to bet one of your teammates will have ridden the horse you've drawn before."

"That's true. I know our team goes to this show every year, so I guess most of the horses will be the same. And I'll also get two warm-up fences, right?"

"Yep, that's right. And you've done a fabulous job riding all of my lesson horses. I think you are more than ready for whatever happens at the show. Now let's go get Penny cooled out and untacked. We have a team meeting tonight, ya' know."

Now that we have listed what to wear, the format of lessons, and class placement, it's time to get down to business and talk about the horse shows.

Major Players

As you've probably started to figure out, IEA shows are run differently than regular hunter/jumper or western shows.

The major players in an IEA show include:

- Show Manager
- Show Secretary
- Judge
- Steward

The show manager is responsible for the operation of the show. This role is usually filled by the coach of the host team.

The show secretary is responsible for the administrative tasks involved in running the show, including:

- Applying for the show date

- Hiring the judge, steward, and EMT

- Creating and distributing the prize lists

- Processing the show entries

- Keeping the official show program

- Collecting entry fees

This role is usually filled by a qualified parent or adult who is a contributing member of the IEA.

The judge is responsible for judging the horse show. Hunt seat judges must hold a United States Equestrian Federation (USEF) judging license and western judges must hold an American Quarter Horse Association (AQHA) or National Reining Horse Association (NRHA) judging license, though a non-licensed judge may be used with the prior written consent of all coaches in the region. In the horse shows, the judge's decision is final.

The steward's job is to interpret the IEA rules and regulations. The steward's major duties include:

- Protecting the interests of exhibitors, judges, and show management

- Investigating and acting upon any alleged rule violations without waiting for a protest

- Granting or denying re-rides

- Supervising the draw
- Determining the suitability of rider to horse, rider to class, and horse to class level

The steward must be at least 21 years of age and meet one of the following criteria:

- Licensed USEF steward
- Current IEA board member or employee
- IEA member coach whose team members are not participating in the competition
- IHSA member coach, who is not otherwise participating in the competition

Required Elements

The required elements of an IEA horseshow include:

- Registration
- Official Schooling
- The Draw
- Coaches Meeting
- Course Walk
- Order of Classes
- Awards Presentation

Registration

The team coaches visit the show office first thing in the morning to check in with the show secretary, confirm that all of their team's entries are correct, pay any outstanding fees, and pick up their coaches packet.

The coaches packet contains a show program, point card, horse description list, copies of the jumping courses (hunt seat) or reining patterns (western), as well as back numbers for the riders (with the exception of Zone 4 in which riders purchase a back number at the beginning of the year that they wear in all regular season competitions). If the team brings horses to the show, the packet will also include their horses' name tags for their saddle pads.

The show program lists the show officials, class schedule, teams competing in the show, and riders by class. You can follow along in the program during the show to determine approximately the time your child will be riding.

The point card is the form the coach uses to designate the team point rider for each class. More information on point cards and scoring can be found in Chapter 7: Points and the Post-Season.

The horse description list provides information on the horses used in the show including horse name, horse provider, physical description, riding description, spur/crop requirements, and any height/weight restrictions.

Official Schooling

All horses used in IEA competitions must be warmed up the day of the show in front of the steward. This designated warm-up session is called the official schooling.

The schooling schedule is organized by fence height with a designated schooling time for each of the three fence levels (2'6", 2', and cross rails). Each horse must school at the highest level at which it will compete. Horses that are entered only in flat classes are required to walk, trot, and canter both directions of the arena. These flat-only horses can complete their required warm up at any time during the official schooling.

At some horse shows the schooling is split into two sessions; morning and afternoon. The horses that are being used in the first half of the day are schooled in the morning and the horses that are used in the second half of the day are schooled once the morning classes have finished. The horses are required to school during only one of the sessions, but the horse owner or steward can request that the horse school in both sessions.

Official schooling

The steward must observe the schooling of all horses entered in the competition and confirm that all over-fences horses have jumped their required height, that the flat-only horses have walked, trotted, and cantered around the ring in both directions, and that all of the horses are appropriate for the classes in which they are entered. The steward also confirms that the spur/crop usage in the morning schooling is consistent with the spur/crop information on the horse description list.

Steward observing morning schooling

Horses must finish their schooling session wearing the tack they will be shown in, including the bit, crop, and spurs. For example, if a horse finishes its schooling session with spurs, the show riders must be given the option of using spurs on that horse. However, if the horse begins schooling with spurs on, but finishes schooling with the spurs off, the horse is not required to be a spur option. In the case of bits, a horse can begin schooling with a stronger bit (like an elevator or a gag) and then be switched to a more show appropriate bit towards the end of its schooling session. The horses must also wear a nametag on their saddle pad so that riders and coaches who are watching the schooling will be able to identify them.

The Draw

The draw is the process in which the riders randomly select the horse they will ride.

There are two types of draw: live draw and steward draw. Both types are legal and which type of draw is used is determined by the show manager. In a live draw, the riders themselves draw the horse they will ride. In a steward draw, the steward and a show management representative draw the horses for the riders.

Riders that compete in more than one class at the horse show (fences and flat for hunt seat or reining and horsemanship for western) draw a different horse for each class in which they compete. A competitor would not ride the same horse in both classes unless she happened to draw the same horse twice.

Coaches Meeting

Once the official schooling is complete, the coaches, steward, and show staff gather in the show office for the coaches meeting, which is usually led by the steward, but can also be run by the show manager or the coach of the host school. During this meeting, the steward passes out copies of the draw; confirms that no height/weight riders drew height/weight restricted horses; goes over the warm-up procedure for over-fences classes; reviews the horse description list, checking the accuracy of the spur/crop designations for each horse and making changes if needed based on the official schooling; and reviews the procedure for requesting a re-ride. At the end of the meeting, the coaches have an opportunity to ask questions or voice any concerns about the horses or the show.

Coaches making notes on the horse description sheet in the coaches meeting

Course Walk

In hunt seat shows, the riders and their coaches walk the fence course on foot to put together a plan for piloting their horse around the course. The course walk generally lasts ten to fifteen minutes.

Course walk

Once the official schooling, draw, coaches meeting, and course walk are complete the show can begin.

Fences Classes

In IEA over-fences classes, the riders complete a course consisting of a minimum of six jumps following a designated order of go. Before competing, the riders are allowed two warm-up fences on the horse that they will be showing. The warm-up can take place in the show arena or outside in a separate practice arena. It is the show manager's decision where the warm-up takes place.

Reining Classes

In IEA reining classes, the riders perform a designated IHSA, AQHA, or NRHA reining pattern. Unlike the over-fences classes, the riders do not get to warm up on the horses prior to showing.

Flat/Horsemanship Classes

In hunt seat equitation on the flat and western horsemanship classes, the riders are asked to walk, trot, and canter (hunt seat) or walk, jog, and lope (western) both directions of the ring in a group. The judge may also ask for additional testing such as sitting trot (hunt seat), two-point position (hunt seat), extended jog (western), ride without stirrups (only novice and above, hunt seat and western), or switch horses. At the conclusion of the class, the riders line up in the center of the ring with their backs to the judge and their placings are called.

Varsity Open Championship Class

The varsity open championship class is an optional class that is not often held at regular season competitions due to time restrictions and sometimes lack of horses.

The class is only offered in the hunt seat discipline and is open only to varsity open riders who qualify based on their placings earlier in the show in the open fences and open flat classes. The top six riders based on combined individual points in the two classes are invited to compete in the championship class. No points are awarded and there is no penalty to the riders or teams if the rider chooses not to compete. It is simply a way to recognize and reward outstanding horsemanship in the varsity open riders. The class has a fence phase and a flat phase.

Championship Western Award

The western equivalent of the hunt seat discipline's varsity open championship class is the championship western award. This is an award issued to the high point rider based on the total of the varsity open horsemanship and varsity open reining points. Unlike the hunt seat varsity open championship, it is not a mounted class, though, in case of a tie, the judge may ask for a ride off between the tied riders. The ride off could be horsemanship or reining and is determined by the judge.

Awards Presentation

At the end of the show day, the official point keepers tabulate the final points and designate the High Point and Reserve High Point Teams for Middle School and High School, as well as a sportsmanship award.

The Sportsmanship Award is given to the competitor who exhibited the most outstanding sportsmanship at the competition. The sportsmanship award recipient may be selected by the steward or show staff or by nomination from coaches and competitors. The method of selection is determined by the show manager prior to the start of the show.

Some show hosts promote good horsemanship and horse care by presenting a Best Turned-Out Horse Award. This award is given to the owner of the horse that is turned out best including grooming, clipping, and overall healthy condition. Like the sportsmanship award, the best turned out horse may be chosen by the steward or show staff or by nomination from coaches and competitors and the method of selection is determined by the show manager.

Awards Table

CHAPTER SEVEN

POINTS AND
THE POST SEASON

"Hey coach, I was looking at the team scoreboard after my crossrail class. I got a fifth, but Becky got a second. The scoreboard says we got two points for the class, but shouldn't we get five points for Becky's placing?"

"Actually Annie, two points is correct because I chose you as our team's point rider for that class. As the point rider, whatever points you get for the class are added to our team point total, even if one of your teammates placed higher than you. Becky will still get her individual points added to her personal total, and she helped our team out too because, by getting second, she blocked another team's point rider from getting those points.

When your child and her teammates go to a horse show, they will be competing both as individuals and as a team during regular season competitions in an effort to qualify for the post season. This chapter describes how individual and team points are accumulated in IEA competitions and how riders and teams advance through the post season from regionals to zones to nationals.

Ribbons and Point Values

Below is the point breakdown for each placing and the corresponding ribbon color:

- First Place = 7 points = blue ribbon
- Second Place = 5 points = red ribbon
- Third Place = 4 points = yellow ribbon
- Fourth Place = 3 points = white ribbon
- Fifth Place = 2 points = pink ribbon
- Sixth Place = 1 point = green ribbon

Some shows also pin a "reserve " placing, which is equivalent to seventh place and has no point value. Sometimes a judge places a rider in reserve to highlight a strong effort worthy of recognition. Some show managers request that the judge pin a reserve rider in each class just in case a rider that placed in first through sixth place is eliminated after the conclusion of the horse show due to an administrative issue, in which case each rider placed below the ineligible rider would move up one placing and the reserve rider would be awarded sixth place and one point.

Individual Points

All riders earn individual points based on their class placings. Each rider is allowed to compete in five regular season shows per year.

18

Once a rider accumulates ~~15~~ points in one class in regular season shows, she is qualified for the first step in the post season, regional finals.

Equitation over fences, equitation on the flat, western horsemanship, and reining are all separate classes and the points are counted separately. A rider must get 15 points in the same class in order to qualify for regionals. Points from two classes cannot be combined to get 15 total points. For example, if a rider gets 5 points in equitation over fences and 7 points in equitation on the flat she can't combine those together to get 12 points.

Also, with regards to points, if a class has twelve or more entrants it may be split into sections. If a class is split, each section must contain at least six riders. Each section is placed individually with first through sixth place ribbons and the corresponding points awarded for each section.

Team Points

Each team designates one rider per division as the team point rider. That rider's team receives team points for her placing in the class and the rider also receives individual points. For example, if the point rider placed second in a class, that rider's team would receive five team points and that rider would receive five individual points.

The team point riders are designated by the coach. The coach selects one rider per class to be their team's designated point rider and indicates their selections on the point card, which is turned in to the show office prior to the draw. A team may have two or more riders in a class, but only the point rider's points count toward the team's point total. All riders' points count toward their individual point total, which determines if they qualify for the post season as an individual, but only the designated point riders' points determine the team's overall placing for that show.

Coaches are required to turn in their point cards prior to the draw so that they cannot select their point riders based on which horses their riders draw.

Throughout the show day, the host team's designated point keeper keeps track of the team points and posts the results of each class on the scoreboard.

At the end of the show, the point keeper totals the points earned by each team's point riders and declares the team with the most points High Point Team for the day and the team with the second most points as Reserve High Point team. All teams receive points based on their placing as a team that day.

The point breakdown for team end of the day placings is shown below.

- High Point Team = 7 points = tri-color ribbon (blue, red, yellow)
- Reserve High Point Team = 5 points = tri-color ribbon (red, yellow, white)
- Third Place Team = 4 points
- Fourth Place Team = 3 points
- Fifth Place Team = 2 points
- Sixth Place Team = 1 point

Sometimes, two or more teams have the same number of points at the end of the day.

In the event of a tie for team points, the following method is used to break the tie:

- Total number of first place finishes

- Total number of second place finishes

- Total number of fence or reining points

If the tie still cannot be determined, the tie is broken by a coin toss.

At the end of the year, all teams who have earned at least 20 team points qualify for the regional high point team competition at regional finals.

Some riders may feel that if they are not the point rider, they are not important to their team. This is not the case. The non-point riders in a class can effectively block other team's point riders from getting points by winning ribbons. For example, if a team has three riders in the class and the point rider is awarded third place, if the other two non-point riders can take first and second place, they can block the other teams' point riders from earning those points.

The Post Season

Riders may qualify for the post season as individuals or as part of their team. There are three separate post season competitions, regional, zone, and national finals, each with an individual and team competition.

Regional Finals

Regional finals consist of both an individual competition that is open to those riders who qualified on an individual basis and a team competition for teams that qualified based on their end of the day placings at regular season shows.

Regional finals are held at the conclusion of the regular season. Only riders from the teams that are assigned to a particular region are allowed to compete in the regional finals.

Classes at regional finals are not split even if there are twelve or more entrants. This is because only a set number of riders from regionals qualify for zone finals. Flat classes may be run in separate heats for safety reasons, but only one set of placings and ribbons is awarded. If a class is run in heats, a certain number of riders from each heat are invited back to compete again in a final class to determine the final placings. For example, if sixteen riders are qualified for regionals in varsity open horsemanship, the class may be run in two heats of eight riders each with the top three, four, or five riders from each of the two heats called back to compete in a final class to determine who moves on to zone finals. Riders re-draw horses for the final class rather than automatically riding the same horse that they rode in the heat because the horses may be used in multiple heats and two or more riders may qualify for the final class on the same horse. Fence and reining classes are run as one class regardless of size because the riders compete one at a time.

The number of riders (for the individual competition) and teams (for the team competition) that move on to zone finals from regionals is determined by the total number of riders in that region. The IEA does its best to make sure the allotment of riders/teams per region allowed at zones is fair based on the size of each region, thus, the reason some regions are allowed to send more riders/teams to zones than other regions.

Zone Finals

Zone finals runs very similarly to regional finals, with a certain number of riders and teams qualified for the show based on their placings in the regional finals. As with regionals, a set number of riders and teams advance to national finals based on their placing at zone finals.

Some zones hold their hunt seat and western zone finals at the same time, while others hold hunt seat and western zone finals on separate weekends. This decision is made by the zone chair, with input from the coaches.

In addition to the actual horse show, many zones also host an end of the year banquet/party for all riders in the zone. Many awards are presented at the banquet including scholarships for sportsmanship and/or service.

National Finals

Just like regional and zone finals, national finals has an individual and team competition that riders and teams must qualify for based on their placings at their zone finals.

Hunt seat and western national finals may be held together, as they were in 2010 in Georgia and 2011 in Maryland, or they may be held separately as in 2012 and 2013 when hunt seat nationals was held in Syracuse, New York and western nationals was held in Oklahoma City, Oklahoma.

In addition to the individual and team competition, several special events also take place at national finals including an exhibitor party, scholarship and sportsmanship awards presentations, and special demonstrations by equine professionals.

CHAPTER EIGHT

A CLOSER
LOOK AT THE DRAW

On the morning of the show Annie approaches Coach with a question. "I saw a lot of ponies schooling this morning. Not that I mind, I think it would be fun to ride a pony, but I'm 5'9". Do you think the judge will take points off my score if I wind up drawing a little pony?"

Coach Kelly, at a stout 5'4", looks up at Annie and smiles. "It's not a problem kiddo. I marked you as a height restricted rider on our entry form, so you aren't eligible to ride a pony. If you draw one by mistake I'll talk to the steward and get an alternate horse for you."

As noted previously, the draw is the process by which the horse each competitor will ride is randomly selected. There are two types of draw: live draw and steward draw. Both types are legal and which type of draw is used is determined by the show manager. In a live draw, the competitors themselves draw the horse they will ride. In a steward draw, the steward and a show management representative draw the horses for the competitors.

The live draw method is used most often in the post-season (regionals, zones and nationals) because it allows for the most transparency in horse draw selection and is fun and exciting for the riders. The steward draw method is used in most regular season competitions because it takes less time and doesn't require the riders to be at the show first thing in the morning.

Height/Weight Restrictions

Prior to the draw, the show manager determines which of the horses are restricted and marks them on the horse grid.

All of the horses fall into one of the categories below:

- Height restricted
- Weight restricted
- Both height and weight restricted
- Neither height nor weight restricted

Ponies (equines that are under 14.2 hands) are considered height restricted. Horses or ponies that are incapable of carrying riders over a specified weight (usually 150 pounds) are considered weight restricted. An equine may be height but not weight restricted (a stout pony), weight but not height restricted (an older 16 hand horse with back or joint soreness issues), or both height and weight restricted (a fine boned pony).

On the other side, the steward may determine that a rider is too small for a horse. If the coach of the rider comes to the steward and asks, the steward can evaluate the height/weight of a rider compared to the horse she has drawn and assign her an alternate horse if necessary (for example a 65 pound 4 foot tall rider on a 16.3 hand warmblood). This is a safety concern more than an aesthetic concern and the final decision rests with the show steward.

A note about height/weight restrictions for riders: the coach is responsible for marking on their entry form all riders with height and/or weight restrictions and this information is available only to the show manager and the steward. Every effort is made to keep this information as confidential as possible to respect the riders' privacy.

Order of Go

In over fences and reining classes the riders compete one at a time and the order of go is randomly drawn. The draw sticks contain the horse's name as well as a number indicating the order of go for the rider that draws that horse.

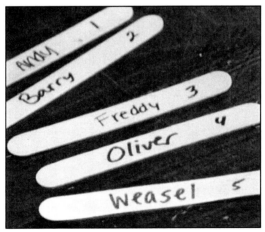

Draw sticks with order of go

The Draw Process

To prepare the draw, the names of the horses are written on individual draw sticks, which can be poker chips, popsicle sticks, the bottom of a cup, or even a slip of paper. If a horse has a height and/or weight restriction, it may be indicated on the draw stick or it may be noted on the steward's draw list. Each class has its own set of draw sticks. For example, if there are ten riders in a class, that class will have ten draw sticks.

To begin, the height and/or weight restricted horse draw sticks are separated from the non–restricted horse draw sticks and the non-restricted horse draw sticks are placed in a hat. The horses for the riders with height and/or weight restrictions are drawn first, while only the non-height/weight restricted horse draw sticks are in the hat. Then the height/weight restricted horse draw sticks are placed back in the hat with the remaining non-height/weight restricted draw sticks and the horses for riders without height/weight restriction are drawn.

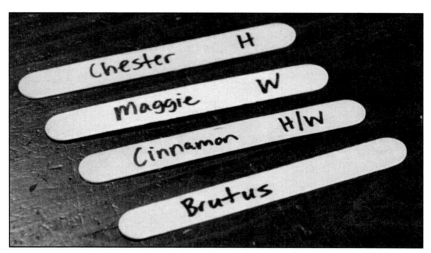

Draw sticks with height/weight restrictions

Riders that compete in more than one class at the horse show (fences and flat for hunt seat or reining and horsemanship for western) draw a different horse for each class in which they compete. A rider would not ride the same horse in both classes unless she happened to draw the same horse twice.

An Example of a Draw

The following is a step-by-step example of a draw for a class of six riders with one height/weight restricted rider, one height restricted rider, and four non-restricted riders:

The steward and all draw attendants have a list of riders with the height/weight restrictions marked, the name of their team, and a blank space to write the horse they draw.

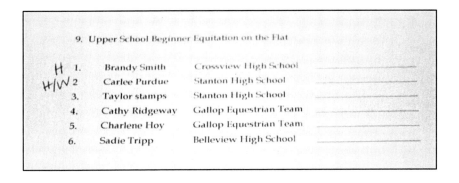

They also have six draw sticks with horse names and height/weight restrictions.

Carlee's horse is drawn first because she is both height and weight restricted. The horses that have a height and/or weight restriction are removed, leaving the three non-restricted horses.

Of these three non-restricted horses, one is drawn for Carlee.

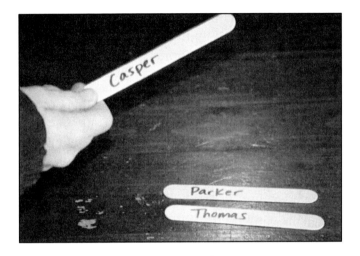

Next, a mount for Brandy, who is height restricted, will be drawn. Starr is placed back in the hat because he is only weight restricted, not height. Bucky and Bruiser are still not in the hat because they are height restricted.

Of these three non-height restricted horses, one is drawn for Brandy.

Then Bucky and Bruiser are placed in the hat along with the other horses that haven't been drawn yet and horses for the remaining riders in the class are drawn.

9. Upper School Beginner Equitation on the Flat				
H	1.	Brandy Smith	Crossview High School	Thomas
H/W	2	Carlee Purdue	Stanton High School	Casper
	3.	Taylor stamps	Stanton High School	Bruiser
	4.	Cathy Ridgeway	Gallop Equestrian Team	Starr
	5.	Charlene Hoy	Gallop Equestrian Team	Parker
	6.	Sadie Tripp	Belleview High School	Bucky

*Please note that for the example above, the draw sticks were shown facing upward so the names of the horses could be seen. This was done for illustrative purposes only. In a real draw, the sticks would be placed in a hat so that the names of the horses could not be seen.

CHAPTER NINE

A CLOSER LOOK AT
THE COACHES MEETING

Annie is standing under her team tent having some hot chocolate and talking with her teammates while they all wait anxiously for Coach Kelly to come out of the coaches meeting with a copy of the draw.

"What's taking so long?" Annie complains as she warms her hands on her cup. "They're been in there for hours! I can't wait to find out which horse I'm riding."

The purpose of the coaches meeting is to get the coaches together with the steward and show manager to discuss how the show will run and make sure the coaches, show manager, steward, and judge are all "on the same page. "

Some people may say the coaches meeting takes a long time just when the riders and parents are anxious to get the show started. However, a thorough coaches meeting that includes discussion of potential issues results in a smoother running show, saving time and frustration in the long run.

After eight years as a steward, I have developed my own coaches meeting script that covers everything I think needs to be discussed. I have outlined my coaches meeting talk below. Please note that there is no IEA rule regarding what must be discussed in the coaches meeting. Other stewards may have more or fewer topics that they choose to address.

Helmets

Helmets must be securely fastened before mounting. An unfastened chin strap can be cause for elimination. Chin straps that can slide in front of the rider's chin while still fastened are too loose and should be tightened. Most stewards choose to "educate rather than eliminate." Personally, I choose to eliminate only if the rider actually enters the ring with the strap unfastened. If it's caught outside the ring I give a stern warning to the student and coach.

Artificial Position Aids

Artificial position aids are illegal in IEA shows. The two most common are "saddle tite" and the "shoulders back" device. "Saddle tite" is a sticky spray or roll-on adhesive that, when applied to a rider's boots or the saddle, provides a little extra "stickiness" to help her hold her legs still. The "shoulders back" device is a harness worn around a rider's shoulders under her hunt coat to help pull her shoulders back and improve her posture. "Saddle tite" and "shoulders back" are brand name products. There are several generic variations on the market that are also illegal.

Tack Adjustments

All tack is legal. Whatever the horse needs to perform at its best is allowed. For example, in IEA competitions it is not unusual for a hunt seat horse to wear a standing martingale in a flat class or a western horse to wear a cavesson in a reining class. Boots and wraps are also allowed for all horses. If a coach feels that a piece of tack is inappropriate (i.e. an excessively harsh bit), he/she may consult with the steward for a ruling.

Girths: only the horse provider or steward may adjust a girth or move a saddle forward.

Stirrups: Riders and coaches may adjust stirrups as needed. The stirrups on hunt seat saddles can be shorted by rolling them; however, the stirrups on western saddles cannot. If the stirrups on a western saddle can't be shorted enough to accommodate a rider, after consulation with the steward and horse provider, the saddle may be replaced. Many western coaches bring spare small saddles to the horse shows just in case there are not enough to go around.

Bridles: Only the horse provider should make adjustments to a bridle. If a coach feels a bridle needs adjusting, he/she should contact the steward who will confer with the horse provider to make any necessary adjustments.

Spur/Crop Use

The horse description sheet lists each horse's specific spur and crop requirements (yes, no, or optional). If the sheet indicates no crop or no spur may be used, then no crop or no spur may be used and use of a crop or spur would be cause for elimination. If the sheet indicates the use of crop or spur is "yes" or "optional," the rider may use a crop or spur, but is not required to do so. However, if a horse is a "yes" or "optional" crop or spur and the rider doesn't use one and cannot get the horse to perform, that is not cause for a re-ride.

As the show day goes on, a horse's spur and/or crop requirements may change. For example, a horse may not need a crop first thing in the morning, but a lower level rider in a later class may need a crop to make the horse canter. If a coach thinks a horse needs a spur/crop and the sheet says no, the coach can request that the steward change the spur/crop requirement. In that case, the steward would consult with the horse owner/representative coach to make a determination. If the spur/crop requirement is changed, then the steward must ensure that all coaches are informed of the change (through a posted notice and/or by announcement over the loud speaker) and all riders who have drawn that horse for the remainder of the day must follow the new spur/crop requirement. No spurs are allowed in the beginner classes (classes 9, 9x, 12, and 12x for hunt seat and classes 4, 4x, 7, and 7x for western)

In hunt seat classes, the spurs are supplied by the horse provider and should be kept with the horse at all times, often attached to the stirrups while the horse is standing in the holding area. Hunt seat riders are expected to provide their own crop, though a horse provider may supply the crop if a horse has a special crop requirement.

In western horsemanship classes, only non-rowelled ball spurs are permitted. During the official warm-up the schooling rider may begin schooling a horsemanship mount with a rowelled spur, but must end the schooling with a ball spur. Western horsemanship riders are expected to provide their own ball spurs (because western spurs come in different sizes depending on the rider's shoe size). If a crop is allowed, it is often supplied by the horse provider because it is very rare for a crop to be used in a western class, usually only in beginner classes where a spur is not permitted, and most western riders do not bring crops to horse shows as standard attire.

Rowelled spurs are allowed in western reining classes under one condition: the rowelled spur worn in the warm up must fit each rider who drew that horse and all riders must use that spur (or they may elect to wear no spur). If the rowelled spur will not fit all of the riders who drew the horse, no one may use a rowelled spur and the horse should be schooled with a ball spur or with no spur, as determined by the horse provider.

During my coaches meeting talk, I run through the horse description list, having each coach confirm yes, no, or optional for spur and crop use for each horse.

Reviewing spur/crop usage in the coaches meeting

Re-Rides

I also discuss re-rides, including the proper procedure and time limit for requesting a re-ride and what happens once a re-ride is granted. A detailed explanation of the re-ride process can be found in Chapter 10: A Closer Look at Re-Rides.

Over Fence Class Warm-Up

The warm-up fences may be in the show ring or in a nearby warm-up ring, as determined by show management. If the warm up is in a separate ring, the riders complete their two fences in the warm up ring, then exit the warm up ring, talk to their coach, and proceed to the show ring. The order of go is drawn for the show ring and should also be followed in the warm up ring. However, the warm up may go out of order if necessary (i.e. a trainer has two riders going first and third and they want to warm them both up at the same time to make things move faster, or a horse is having a tack issue that must be resolved so the next rider moves ahead in the line to save time).

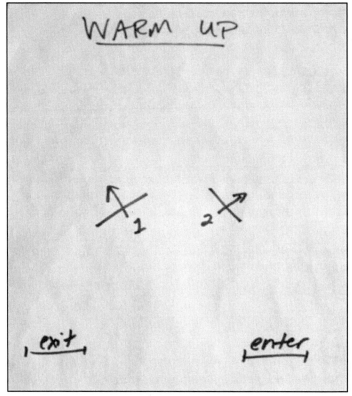

An example of a warm up course

If the warm up is in the show ring, it may be conducted one of two ways. The first option is to have each rider do her two warm up jumps, return to the in-gate, speak with her coach for 30 seconds, then jump the course. The second option is to have several riders (usually about six) do their warm up jumps one after the other. Each rider exits the ring when they have completed their warm up and when the entire group is done, the first rider re-enters the ring and jumps her course, then the second rider, etc. While the show manager has the final say on which option is chosen, I always ask the coaches in the coaches meeting to get their consensus.

The Draw

After confirming that all coaches have turned in their point cards, I pass out the draw and indicate any changes to the draw based on schooling if the draw was done beforehand. Then I give the coaches time to review the draw and let me know if there are any issues (i.e. a height/weight rider has drawn a restricted horse, an exceptionally small rider has drawn a large horse, or a beginner rider has drawn a horse that cannot be ridden without spurs).

A coach marking her riders on the show program

Questions/Comments?

Once I've concluded my talk, I ask the coaches if they have any questions or anything related to the show that they would like to discuss. For example, a coach may ask for clarification from the judge regarding his/her preference for simple or flying changes in the reining pattern. If a coach has a question for the judge, I ask the judge and report back to all of the coaches. Once all issues are addressed, the meeting is adjourned and we head out to the arena to start the show.

CHAPTER TEN

A CLOSER
LOOK AT RE-RIDES

"What just happened? Did you see that?" Coach Kelly glances from the arena over to the coach next to her.

"He just stopped. Everything was fine and then he just stopped. It all happened so quickly," the other coach replies.

Annie is still astride her horse, but barely. She looks over her shoulder at Coach Kelly standing by the in-gate as she rights herself in the saddle and begins to circle back around to attempt the cross rail again.

"Pick up your canter, left lead, make a circle and try again, Annie. Keep pushing him all the way to the fence." Coach Kelly instructs her student from the rail while making her way to the steward.

"Steward, I would like a re-ride," Coach Kelly states.

IEA competition is unique in that the riders compete on a borrowed horse and only the riders' abilities, not the horses', are being judged. Sometimes, to insure that a rider can be fairly judged using this format, a re-ride is necessary.

The decision-making process for re-rides is more art than science. The steward is tasked with watching the entire show, confirming that all rules are followed, and making sure all of the horses are performing adequately. It's a big job to say the least. Incidents happen in the blink of an eye and it can be difficult to determine the exact cause on the spot.

In this chapter I will explain what a re-ride is, how it is requested, and what is done with the original horse if a re-ride is granted.

From the Rulebook

Let's begin by reviewing the rulebook definition of a re-ride. The bold print below is lifted from the 2013-2014 IEA rulebook:

When through no fault of the rider, a horse performs so poorly that it is impossible to fairly judge the rider's ability, a re-ride may be granted.

The first thing to note here is that the issue (be it a buck, missed lead, stop at a fence, refusal to spin in a reining class, or any other issue for which the re-ride is requested) must have occurred by the horse through no fault of the rider.

Secondly, the horse's performance must be so poor that the rider cannot be fairly judged. Sometimes a horse has a minor disobedience in a flat or rail class (a small buck, a spook in a corner, etc.) that the rider handles well. In these cases, the steward will radio to the judge to see if he/she can "judge through" the incident as if it never happened and proceed with the class.

If the judge feels that he/she can judge through the incident, then the class proceeds as if the incident never occurred. If the judge feels that he/she cannot fairly judge through the incident and the steward feels that the incident was not caused by the rider, the steward will grant a re-ride.

If the horse is lame (not serviceably sound) the steward will grant a re-ride.

A re-ride must be requested before the lineup in a flat class or the last horse leaves the ring in an over fences class.

In flat and horsemanship classes, re-rides must be requested prior to the lineup because once the horses have lined up, the judge has often already pinned the class and the judge, steward, and show staff have already moved on to the next class.

For fences and reining classes, the re-ride must be requested before the last rider leaves the ring. If a rider is third in a class of eight, the coach of the third rider has until the eighth rider leaves the ring to request a re-ride. This is especially helpful for the steward if the horse goes twice in the same class because the steward can evaluate the horse with a second rider to see if the same incident happens with another rider (stop, spook, etc.). I always give the coach of the last rider in a class a few extra seconds to get to me to request the re-ride so they don't feel like they have to run over to me while their rider is still on course or on pattern.

Only the coach of the rider involved may request a re-ride.

This bears repeating. Only the coach may request a re-ride, not a parent, another rider on the team, or the actual rider while in the class (it has happened…). The second important point here is that that the coach must actually request a re-ride. If the steward or the judge sees a dangerous situation arising (for example, a horse about to get upset and begin bucking in a flat class) either of them have the option of stopping the class due to safety issues, but in order for a re-ride to take place, the coach must request it.

When a coach makes a request, she must state her request directly, "steward, I would like a re-ride" rather than just implying that they would like a re-ride, "hey look at that one, it sure looks upset to me," or "wow, that was a dirty stop don't you think?" etc.

The exception to this rule is in the case of lameness. The steward may retire a lame horse and provide the rider with an alternate without waiting for a re-ride request.

Although they may confer with show management and the judge, only the steward may grant or deny a re-ride.

It is the steward's job to grant or deny re-rides. I often confer with the judge to get an educated and unbiased second opinion, but when it comes down to it, it's my responsibility and the buck (no pun intended) stops with me.

The steward's decision is final. If a coach disagrees with the steward's decision, she may file a protest at the conclusion of the show asking for further review by the Zone Ethics Committee and the national steward.

If a re-ride is granted in a class in which riders compete individually (over fences, reining, or workout classes), it shall be judged as if the first ride never occurred and the re-ride shall take place after all other rides in that class have been completed.

If a re-ride is granted in a class in which riders compete together (flat, horsemanship, or performance classes), it will be the Judge's discretion whether to restart the class from the beginning or resume the class from the point when it was stopped.

The decision on whether to start a class over from the beginning or pick back up where the re-ride took place is up to the judge. For example, if a lameness occurs while tracking right in a flat class, the judge may choose to only re-run the class to the right.

During a competition, if it is determined by the sole determination of the show officials who witnessed the event that a rider fell from the horse through no fault of the rider and due instead to the unexpected and unanticipated actions of the horse being ridden, the rider shall be granted a re-ride.

A re-ride is not automatically granted after a fall. Just like any other situation, the coach must request a re-ride from the steward.

The Re-Ride Process

If the re-ride occurred during a fence class, the rider completes her two warm up fences and her competition round from the beginning on the new horse. If the re-ride occurred during a reining class, the rider starts the reining pattern over from the beginning on the new horse. For flat and horsemanship classes, the judge decides whether the class is re-run from the beginning or if it is re-started where the re-ride occurred.

Steward consulting her notes regarding a re-ride request

The Horse

If a re-ride is granted, the original horse may or may not be pulled from the competition for the remainder of the day. With the exception of lameness, it is the steward's decision whether to keep or pull the horse. If the horse is lame (not serviceably sound) it is pulled from the show for the remainder of the day.

If the re-ride was not due to unsoundness in the horse, the steward may choose to have the horse re-schooled to see if its behavior can be corrected and it can be reasonably assumed that the horse will perform adequately if left in the show. For example, if a tent blew over and spooked the horse causing it to stop at the fence, the horse may be fine once the tent is removed and the horse is re-schooled. If the horse continues to perform poorly with the schooling rider, the steward will pull the horse from the remainder of its classes.

Sometimes a horse's behavior may be considered suitable for an upper level rider, but not for a lower level rider. Riders in upper level classes (such as intermediate and open) are expected to have the skills to handle a more difficult horse than novice or beginner riders. Thus, if a re-ride is requested in an upper level class and the steward does not feel that a re-ride is warranted, the steward may still choose to pull the horse from its lower level classes even though a re-ride was not granted in the upper level class.

ACKNOWLEDGMENTS

This book would not be possible without the help of a great many people. I'd first like to thank my very supportive parents who have always encouraged me to follow my dreams. I love you!

Many thanks to my review committee: Roxane Lawrence, Myron Leff, Casey Dunn, Betsy Aliffi, Katie Poteet, Eileen Stone, Wendy Benevides, and Simon Towns, who labored through version after version of this manuscript providing so much insight and a shoulder to lean on.

I'd also like to thank the IEA administrative staff, including Roxane Lawrence, Myron Leff, Stephanie Keough, Jennifer Eaton, and Kathryn Quinlin for allowing me to play a small part in an amazing organization. I've never met a group of people who find more joy in a succession of 16-hour days filled with hard physical labor and mental stress, made possible only by an ample supply of laughter, camaraderie, and diet coke (I am, of course, referring to IEA hunt seat and western national finals) except maybe my horse managing partner, Ashley Wilson.

Oh my goodness, Ashley Wilson. Where would I be without you? From student who tried to run me over in the arena in her first IHSA lesson (did you think I forgot about that?), to star open western rider (with a shiny belt buckle to prove it), to confidante and friend. You've been there from the start of my professional career and I am so grateful for our friendship.

I'd also like to say thank you to photographer Kensie Arnold for taking such great pictures and editing them over and over at my whim. Big things are in store for you. I can't wait to see what your future brings.

Thank you also to the good folks at Pine Lane Farm in Conyers, Georgia, for acting as photo models: Amelia Stone, Lindsey Benton, Lilly Nowak, Lydia Roberts, Emily Wold, Elana Wolkan, Kristin Oliver, and Katie Poteet. The hardest part was choosing the best photos from so many good ones. And thank you to Doug Dershimer, horse show dad and amateur photog extraordinaire who filled in with some last minute pictures when the weather didn't cooperate for a scheduled horse show shoot with Kensie.

I'd like to express a million thanks to Casey Dunn (alias Jadie Jones), published author, IEA coach, and friend, for sharing your knowledge and wisdom. Just a year ago, this manuscript was only a collection of notes on my hard drive, destined never to see the light of day until Casey encouraged me to organize my thoughts, get them on paper, and (gasp!) talk to Roxane. I could never have done this without you (and our late night online chat sessions, lol).

And lastly, I must thank the IEA coaches, riders, and parents I've interacted with over the years. This book is the product of everything I've learned from you. I'm so grateful to be a steward.

ABOUT THE AUTHOR

Amanda Garner is an Interscholastic Equestrian Association (IEA), Intercollegiate Horse Show Association (IHSA), and Georgia Hunter Jumper Association (GHJA) steward, a schooling show judge, and the head coach of the University of North Georgia IHSA Equestrian Team. She is also the owner of Epiphany Farm, LLC in Dahlonega, Georgia, where she resides with her many horses and her cat, Chewy.

If you have any comments or suggestions for future versions of this book I'd love to hear from you. Please contact me through my website www.Epiphany-Farm.com or if our paths cross at a horse show, feel free to stop and say hello.